What Do Historians Do?

Brenda Parkes

Historians study
what happened in the past.
Some historians study
the lives of pioneers.

Historians look at pictures
of pioneers.

They look at homes to see
how pioneers lived.

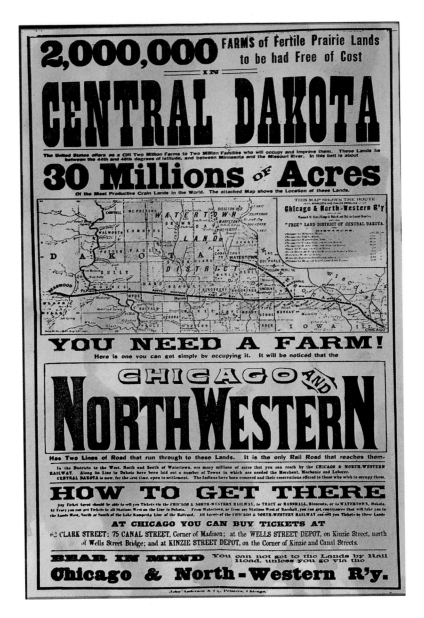

Historians read what pioneers wrote.

They look at tools
that pioneers used.

Historians share what they learned.
Museums show things pioneers used.

Books tell about pioneers.

We can be historians, too.
We can visit places to learn
about pioneers.

We can see how pioneers lived.

We can read books about pioneers.

We can write about pioneers, too.

We can make models of things
pioneers used.

We can share what we learned.